W9-DFY-996

The Civilization Library
Published in the United States by
Gloucester Press in 1978

All rights reserved
Originated and designed by
Judith Escreet,
David Cook Assoc.,
produced by
The Archon Press Ltd
28 Percy Street
London W1P 9FF

First published in
Great Britain 1978 by
Hamish Hamilton
Children's Books Ltd
90 Great Russell Street
London WC1B 3PT

The publishers wish to acknowledge
the assistance received from
William Lancaster
during the preparation of this book.

Printed in Great Britain by
W. S. Cowell Ltd
Butter Market, Ipswich

Library of Congress Cataloging in Publication Data

Lancaster, Fidelity.
    The Bedouin.

    (The Civilization library)
    Includes index.
    SUMMARY: Describes the life, history, customs,
and changing world of the two and one half million
Arabic-speaking nomads in Syria, Iraq, Jordan, other
countries of the Arabian peninsula, and North Africa.
    1. The Bedouins—Juvenile literature. [1. Bed-
ouins] I. Wilson, Maurice Charles John, 1914– II.
Title. III. Series.
DS36.9.B4L36   1978   953'.05   78–2679
ISBN 0–531–01447–9

THE CIVILIZATION LIBRARY

THE BEDOUIN

Fidelity Lancaster

William Lancaster, Consultant

Illustrated by

Maurice Wilson

Gloucester Press | New York | 1978

Desert nomads

The Bedouin and religion

The Bedouin are Muslims, like most of the townspeople of the area. But they are independent in their practice of religion, as in everything else. Most say the five daily prayers and fast during the holy month of Ramadan.

Dependence and independence

Only Salubba families stayed in the inner desert all year. With their small donkey herds, they could use shallow wells. The Bedouin moved to oases or to villages for the summer.

"God sends the rain so that the herds will have pasture. From the herds we shall have milk to drink, hair for our tents, and young to sell for grain and coffee. In the desert we are free," say the Bedouin.

This description of Bedouin life is basically true. The Bedouin are Arabic-speaking nomads; they travel the desert, moving from place to place, to find food for themselves and their herds. The townspeople give them the name "Bedouin"—desert-dweller. Most of the tribes or groups of Bedouin are camel herders, but some herd sheep and goats. Today there are about 2½ million Bedouin spread through Syria, Iraq, Jordan, and the other countries of the Arabian peninsula and North Africa.

The Bedouin have been herding camels since about 1000 B.C. Before that, the desert was inhabited by people with donkeys. Camels, like donkeys, can survive in the inner desert. Sheep and goats cannot, and so the tribes that herd these animals stay on the edges of the desert.

There are other nomadic groups in the desert. The Salubba are probably descended from an earlier desert people. Other groups have special skills like blacksmithing, metalworking and repairing, and trading.

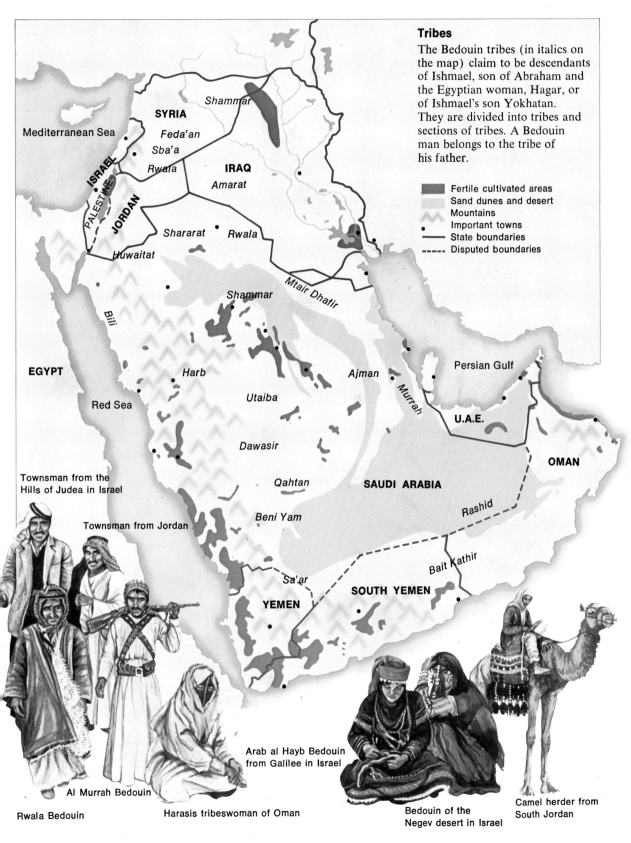

Tribes

The Bedouin tribes (in italics on the map) claim to be descendants of Ishmael, son of Abraham and the Egyptian woman, Hagar, or of Ishmael's son Yokhatan. They are divided into tribes and sections of tribes. A Bedouin man belongs to the tribe of his father.

- Fertile cultivated areas
- Sand dunes and desert
- Mountains
- • Important towns
- —— State boundaries
- ---- Disputed boundaries

Mediterranean Sea

SYRIA

Shammar

Feda'an

Sba'a

Rwala

ISRAEL

PALESTINE

JORDAN

IRAQ

Amarat

Shararat

Rwala

Huwaitat

Bili

Shammar

Mtair Dhafir

EGYPT

Harb

Utaiba

Ajman

Murrah

Persian Gulf

U.A.E.

Red Sea

Dawasir

Qahtan

SAUDI ARABIA

OMAN

Beni Yam

Rashid

Bait Kathir

Sa'ar

SOUTH YEMEN

YEMEN

Townsman from the Hills of Judea in Israel

Townsman from Jordan

Al Murrah Bedouin

Rwala Bedouin

Harasis tribeswoman of Oman

Arab al Hayb Bedouin from Galilee in Israel

Bedouin of the Negev desert in Israel

Camel herder from South Jordan

5

Camel herders

Perennial desert plants

Perennial plants live on from year to year; they have root systems to store moisture.

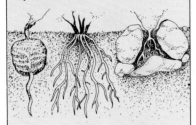

Surviving in the desert

Below are seeds of annual plants. Annuals flower, produce seeds, and die within a year. The seeds are protected by an outer coat that dissolves and allows them to germinate, or sprout, only when there is enough rain.

Coated seed   Uncoated seed

Annual flowers

Buttercup

Anemone

Buckthorn   Mountain knot grass

The camel herder's life is hard, but it is independent and free. The camels set the pattern of life. When the bright star Canopus appears in the night sky (October to November), the herders begin to find out where rain has fallen, and how much. From the reports of rain, they can tell where there will be grazing pasture for the camels, and whether it will be good. Knowledge of the desert and its plants, and the ability to find good pasture make a successful herder.

While a family moves from an area of poor grazing to reach a better one, life is very hard. The family and herd travel 25 to 30 miles (40 to 50 km) a day. Just enough of the tent is set up to cover the children, and there is no cooked food, only camel milk and flour mixed with milk. Most years the herding families travel about 770 miles (or 1200 km) between winter grazing and summer watering places. But when they reach good pasture, they can rest and visit other families.

One family can usually manage a herd of forty to fifty camels; the men care for the animals, the women look after the tent and the people. If a family loses a member and can't manage, it may join another short-handed family. The families are nearly always related. Bedouin get help from groups of relatives bound together by common ancestors. More distant relatives are drawn into the group by marriage.

Camel-herding families seem poor but consider themselves comfortable. Their herds and tents are valuable, although their cash earnings are small. Camels breed slowly, and there are few buyers for them. Raising sheep, or working for an oil company or in the military services brings in money. Spare cash is used for a truck, land, or more camels or sheep. Like everyone else, the Bedouin want to protect and provide for their children, and camels are thought of as savings. They are the basis of the Bedouin's livelihood, for even in the harsh desert, they can always subsist.

Livelihood

A family can survive on fifteen camels and is well-off with fifty. A milk camel is worth well over $500, a trained baggage camel over $400, and a riding camel up to $1,900 or more. The tent, bedding, and cooking equipment cost at least $1,300. The family earns money from selling camels' milk, camels' hair, and young male camels.

Desert spring

Camels' milk for breakfast

—and for every other meal! Milk is the basic food of the camel herders and, for long periods, they may have little else. Since camels have milk for eighteen months after giving birth, the camel herders don't need to preserve the milk by making it into cheese or dried yogurt. They just salt the milk in the morning. This stops it from turning sour during the day. Camels' milk has a very high vitamin C content. In the spring there are other foods available too. After heavy rains edible fungus plants called truffles are easy to find and dig up. They are boiled or baked in ashes. Eggs, usually from sand grouse, are made into omelets or boiled. Bulbs and some roots are eaten raw in salads.

Spring is the Bedouin's favorite season. If winter rains have fallen, then in spring the desert is green. The grasses are knee high; the bushes send out new shoots; lizards dart through the flowers; mother camels drip milk while their fluffy coated young gambol about them. The year will be good. And even if there is no rain the following winter, the grass will be good for hay, and the bushes will be good for still another year.

A green spring means the camels will be strong for the summer. The mares and foals drink milk, as do the dogs. The women comb loose hair from the camels and begin spinning. Children hunt bulbs, roots, birds' eggs, jerboas, and lizards; and they chase rabbits with the salukis—a kind of hunting dog. Women and children gather truffles. In some areas the men who are out with the grazing camels find the semh plant growing; its seeds can be ground into flour. Sometimes at the end of spring swarms of locusts appear. The people dig ditches along the insects' path and

then build large, smoky fires to drive the insects into the ditches. Fried locusts taste like spinach; but most are dried and ground into flour.

Spring doesn't arrive by the calendar. It is an event that depends on rain. Some areas have spring; others go straight from winter to summer. If there is spring over most of the desert, the Bedouin tents are scattered. If spring is not widespread, the tents are crowded together in the areas of good grazing. When the grazing land is used up, the men of each tent decide where to move next.

Spring used to be the season for raiding, so people of a tribe moved as a group for protection. Now each family plans its own migration. They consider the quality of the grazing land on the way to different wells, which wells have working water pumps, where they might meet families to arrange marriages, and where there are feuding families. Sometimes they need their sheik's advice or help, so they spend the summer near his well.

Salukis
Most camel herders have one or two of these sleek desert greyhounds. They are used mainly for hunting rabbits. The great sheiks hunted gazelles with hawks and salukis; the dogs rode on camels until the gazelles were found.

Eating jerboas
Jerboas are small desert rodents that live in holes. Children dig them out for the salukis to catch. The jerboas are roasted and shared with the dogs.

Houses of hair

The Bedouin call their tents "houses of hair," for they are made of goats' or camels' hair that is woven into heavy fabric strips about 65 feet (21 m) long and 3 feet (1 m) wide. The strips are sewn together. One very large piece, made of eight or ten strips, is used for the roof. Its ends hang down to form the two side walls of the tent. The front and back walls are made of two other large pieces. Most tents have a floor space of 30 or 40 feet (10 or 12 m) by 12 or 15 feet (4 or 5 m). Some are smaller, and a wealthy family's might be even larger.

Camel herders usually buy goats' hair strips for the tent roof since it is best for keeping out water. When it rains, the goats' hair absorbs water and swells, so the tent becomes waterproof. Front and back walls are of woven hair from the herders' own camels; camels' hair is more wind resistant. The men used to make rope from camels' hair, but now they buy it. The tent poles are poplar wood;

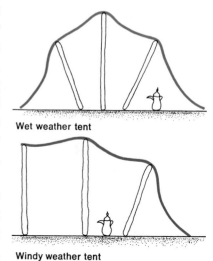

Wet weather tent

Windy weather tent

Putting up the tent
It takes about an hour to lay out the tent and ropes, hammer in the pegs, attach and tighten the ropes, put up the poles, and tighten the ropes again.

the pegs that hold the ropes are iron or tamarisk wood.

The tents work well in the changing weather of the desert. In summer, the poles are raised to their highest, side walls are tied up, front and back walls are left unpinned. In winter, front and back walls are tied down, poles are lowered to offer less wind resistance, and fires are lit.

Inside, a woven curtain hangs across the middle of the tent to divide it into the men's side and the women's side. In the men's part of the tent are the fire, the coffee equipment, a gun, and perhaps a light. Everything else—rugs, quilts, mattresses, pillows, extra clothes, and a folded up loom—is piled on the women's side. Bunches of herbs and a knife hang from the roof, and so may a baby's hammock. Near the front wall is a cooking fireplace. At the side are cooking equipment and sacks of food. Firewood or camel dung to be used as fuel is piled outside, and the water bag is kept in the shade nearby.

Tent repairs

The Bedouin women take the tent apart and resew it every year. They do this before the winter storms, usually at the end of summer when there are other women nearby to help. Two new strips are sewn into the center of the roof section, and the old strips are moved toward the ends. The old edge strips are used for patches. The bottom strips of the front and back walls need replacing every year.

Water from the wells

If spring is good, the camels do not need to be watered. But in the summer, as the grazing dries out, the herders have to take the camels for water. About every five days they go to rain pools, shallow wells, or water basins in the rocks. Water is more important than grazing. The camels can live on the fat stored in their humps, but they need water every few days.

Now there are new wells in the desert—drilled by the government or with government help. Sometimes there is a small charge for the water. It is pumped from the well into concrete basins and small canals that are laid out. This way many camels can drink at one time without spoiling the water. Sheep and goats have their own basins. There are pools where people can fill cans and water bags with drinking water, and there is a large pool where trucks can be filled with water for the flocks of sheep out in the desert.

In the middle of summer the wells are busy all day and all night, especially the wells of the sheiks who don't charge

for water. The sheik of a tribe has a permanent tent and house at the well drilled under his protection. Other members of each tribe also own wells and share the water within their group. In the past, each part of a tribe dug shallow wells, but these dried up in summer.

Many herders like to water their animals in the cool of dusk or dawn, and they spend the night talking with other herders or at the sheik's tent. The herds rest nearby. Trucks arrive packed with barrels, tanks, and small boys. The boys fill the tanks, then stand under the pumps themselves playing in the water. Girls wash more quietly, at the edges of the pools, and then they carry water pans back to their tents. Camel herds arrive and grumblingly wait their turn for water. Small girls collect sacks of dung for fuel. Some straying camels mix with a sheep herd. The angry shepherd shouts for the camel herder who comes running, yelling and driving his animals away with a stick. Tempers are quick in the heat.

Summer water

Before the new, deep wells were drilled, camel herders camped at oases (fertile areas) near villages that had old wells on the edges of the desert. They stayed just outside the villages. The young men took the camels in every three days to be watered and brought back a supply of water for the tents. The Bedouin did not like summer. It was hard on the camels, and camping in crowded areas meant disease and dirt. They longed for rain so they could return to the clean desert.

Feasts and celebrations

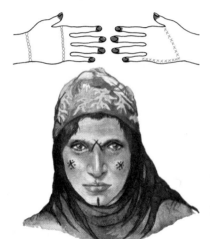

Henna and tattooing

Many girls and women tattoo their faces and hands. A dye made from the henna plant is used on the palms of the hands; men may dye their hair with it to show that they have been to Mecca.

Feasts are held for visiting relatives, to celebrate weddings, and to honor the dead at the end of the Moslem holy month of Ramadan. After a wedding, the host (the bridegroom or his father) kills a sheep or camel in front of his tent. This is an invitation to the men of the tribe. They gather in the host's tent which has been spread with rugs and cushions. The most honored guests sit with their backs to the dividing curtain. Coffee and tea are served, and the guests trade news.

The host tells the women when the guests are ready for food. Huge trays are piled with rice, barley, or flat sheets of bread. Sheep or camel meat is placed on top, and gravy is poured over the meat. The guests eat while the bridegroom makes fresh tea and heats coffee. The men of the tent eat after the guests. The trays are sent back to the women who scoop the food into dishes and carry it to neigh-

boring tents. The bride's mother has eaten earlier, but the other women of the tent eat last.

Marriages are usually arranged by the parents, but the first moves are made by the young man. The men of the two families agree that the marriage would be a good idea; then the women settle the details. All the parents want the marriage to last, so they will not force a young woman to marry someone she does not like; that would be shameful. If the tribe is near a town, a religious official can perform the wedding. The feast is held afterward.

Usually, the young people are already related. The Bedouin feel this ties two groups of related people even closer together, so the opportunities of both groups are multiplied. The Bedouin say marriage is for the sake of children. It provides for the future of the group and gives the children the best protection and economic advantage.

Wedding feast
The guests have been served plates of meat with bread or rice. The bride, seated on a rug at the women's side of the tent, shares her meal with some of the younger children.

Midsummer

Midsummer in the desert is a little like midwinter in the United States. Plant life dies down or stops growing. Some animals dig burrows or find holes where they stay (just as some animals hibernate in winter) until the hottest time is over. Other animals and most birds migrate to cooler areas. In the past, the Bedouin and their herds migrated also—to oases or villages on the edge of the desert that had good, permanent water supplies. Each tribe or section of a large tribe returned to the same village every summer. In a way, they belonged to that village. They protected it from raids of other tribes, and in return the village provided them with grain or dates. The only people left in the inner desert were the Salubba who could survive because their herds were very small—and so needed little water—and because they had great knowledge of the desert.

Now there are new, deep wells in the desert, so the Bedouin stay there. But they move northward or onto higher desert ground. Even there, it is often over 113° F (45° C)

Visits from traders

Traders from the villages where the tribes used to camp for the summer now come to them in the desert by truck bringing barley, flour, vegetables, and fruit to sell. Each tribe or section of a tribe also has a permanent merchant whose family has traded with them for generations. The merchant has a shop in the sheik's permanent camp, and he sells tent material, poles and rope, clothing, bedding, food staples, and cooking and herding equipment.

Summer food

In summer, the young camels drink all the camel milk. People eat vegetable stews with rice or barley and salads with bread. Tomatoes, onions, and peppers are eaten too, but the Bedouin prefer their winter diet.

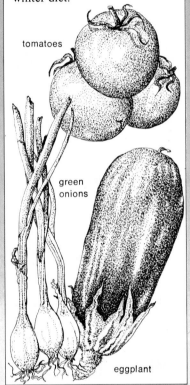

tomatoes

green onions

eggplant

during the day. The nights are cooler, about 86° F (30° C), and there is sometimes a breeze in the late afternoon.

In summer the camps are very large, sometimes a thousand tents are set up in one area. The Bedouin stay until cooler weather and autumn rains arrive. The young men take the herds out to graze and come back every few days for water. The older men visit friends and relatives and sit in the sheik's tent. Since many different families are in the same place, arguments can be settled and business deals completed. There is time to visit the town, to take care of licenses, and to attend to other matters. And the sheik is on hand to give advice.

The women visit and collect information to use in planning marriages. They do their work in the early morning or evening. The spinning is nearly finished, and weaving begins. Children become cross and short-tempered with the heat and the change of diet. Before the camp breaks up, the women help each other resew their tents.

Weaving

Tribal patterns

Each tribe and section of a tribe has favorite patterns. Weavers in camel-herding tribes use finer thread, fewer colors, and simpler patterns than weavers in sheep-herding tribes. The patterns below are (from the top) Negev Bedouin, South Jordan Bedouin, and Dhiyabat Bedouin.

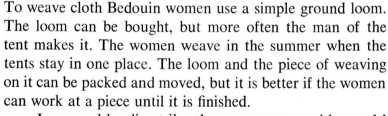

To weave cloth Bedouin women use a simple ground loom. The loom can be bought, but more often the man of the tent makes it. The women weave in the summer when the tents stay in one place. The loom and the piece of weaving on it can be packed and moved, but it is better if the women can work at a piece until it is finished.

In a camel-herding tribe, the women weave with camels' hair. In sheep- and goat-herding tribes, they use sheep's wool and goats' hair and white cotton that they buy. As a rule, new cloth for tent walls and grain sacks is woven each year. The wool is spun rather thick and left in natural colors of brown, white, and black. The easiest pattern is used for sacks and tent walls. It has stripes that run the length of

18

the piece. The women also weave beautiful dividing curtains, rugs for wedding gifts, saddle bags, and small bags used as both pillows and carryalls for extra sets of clothes. These are made of finely woven wool that is dyed dark blue, green, red, or yellow. The designs for these are more interesting, and every woman has her own version of her tribe's patterns.

From 1958 through 1962 there was a great drought and many camels died. Some Bedouin families gave up camel herding. Some families now settle in towns at least for the years of their children's schooling. For these reasons, less weaving is done. But many settled families keep woven dividing curtains and other pieces as reminders of the past.

Weaving a dividing curtain

The curtain that separates the women's side of the tent from the men's side is made of three or four long strips of material sewn together. The top two strips are patterned. The bottom strip, or strips, are made of good quality tent cloth.

19

The sheik

The sheik advises

A member of the tribe complains to the sheik that a year earlier he had sent his sheep to a shepherd. Now he wants them back, but the shepherd says they have all died. The men listening laugh. The sheik asks the man if he checked on his sheep during the year. The man answers that he did not. The sheik becomes annoyed and tells the man he is a fool; people who don't look after their sheep deserve to lose them. At sessions like these, everyone listens and gives advice. Common sense usually rules.

The head of the tribe is the sheik, a man known for courage, generosity, and skill in settling problems. The office of sheik is held by one family, and the position goes to the family member best suited to be sheik. A son doesn't always become sheik after his father, or brother after brother. In the past, there were bloody fights or even splits in a tribe over who would follow a sheik.

Other tribe members take no part in a power struggle in the sheik's family. They just hope for a good sheik—one who can settle arguments and protect and lead them in times of trouble. This used to mean leading the tribe in war; now it means acting as ambassador for the tribe in the world of governments. The sheik deals with the government on ques-

tions of rights to drill new oil wells, or rents for oil pipelines that cross a tribe's land, or jobs at government centers or frontier posts. The sheik helps tribe members in disputes over camels or broken marriage promises. He helps men get work and money to educate their sons. Sometimes villagers or townsmen come to the sheik too. Women ask help of the sheik's wife or mother.

To be successful, a sheik must be more generous and honorable than anyone else. He has no real power. His decisions are accepted only if he is respected. A hundred years ago the sheik of a large tribe said, "I cannot lead my tribe: I can only lead them where they want to go." This is still true today.

Making coffee
Fresh coffee is made every morning by the men. The beans are roasted over a fire, then pounded in a wooden or brass bowl. Coffee is served in brass pots, unsweetened but flavored with the spice cardamon. Guests are offered coffee as a sign of hospitality. (The host is always the one to prepare it.) In return, guests must behave with honor.

A free Bedu

Bedouin men have few possessions—a riding camel or truck, a gun, some clothes. Tents and things in them belong to women. The herd a man cares for belongs to his sons, or his brother's sons if he has none of his own. Among Bedouin, birth and reputation are more important than wealth. From his birth as a member of an independent, camel-herding tribe, a man is a free Bedu, and there is nothing higher. The Bedouin say honor comes through women, and it is developed through a mother's care and her teaching of Bedouin virtues to her children.

A man's reputation is also earned through his actions from childhood on. If he is courageous and generous, he is liked and respected. He is given responsibility early and counted on for difficult tasks. In the past, he would have been taken on raiding parties. Young men built their own stock of animals by raiding the herds of others. A man known to be a successful raider would be welcomed into any group as a brother-in-law. Now, young men start out by earning money working for an oil company, by trading, or in the military service.

Camel raiding

Camel raids were usually carried out by small groups of young men trying to start herds of their own. They raided the herds of distant tribes. Herds that were too big to be well guarded would be attacked, and some of the camels would be taken. Young men had a chance to make their reputations as successful raiders. Now the governments have stopped the practice of raiding.

A day out

In the past, the Bedouin used to sell many horses and young male camels to traders. Female camels that produced no young were sold as meat. Most of the horses were shipped to India. The young male camels were trained and sent to cities throughout the Middle East to be used for transport.

In the 1920s and 1930s, cars and trucks began to be used, and the Bedouin could no longer sell their camels and horses for good prices. During this time, the young men often joined the Camel Corps, or the Bedouin Legion of the armed services of any country they found themselves in. They still do this, but now they can find other jobs too.

Today, in countries with little land suited for farming, the government often helps sheep and camel herders. Many of the herding families have trucks. In late summer or early winter, the family loads their truck with extra camels and takes them to the butcher shop in the village. The whole family goes along.

There are many new towns and villages with markets along the oil pipelines and highways. A market is made up of a row or square of small shops with stands in front of them. Some sell food, fruit, and vegetables. Others have herding equipment, tools, lamps, water barrels, and spare parts for trucks. The Bedouin can also buy tent material, bedding, and clothing here.

In town, the men take care of government matters and deal with the camels while the women look in the shops. If the men have gotten a good price for the camels, they buy clothes, grain, dates, rice, sugar, tea, coffee, and tent material. If they have money left over, the children get candy, fruit, and nuts.

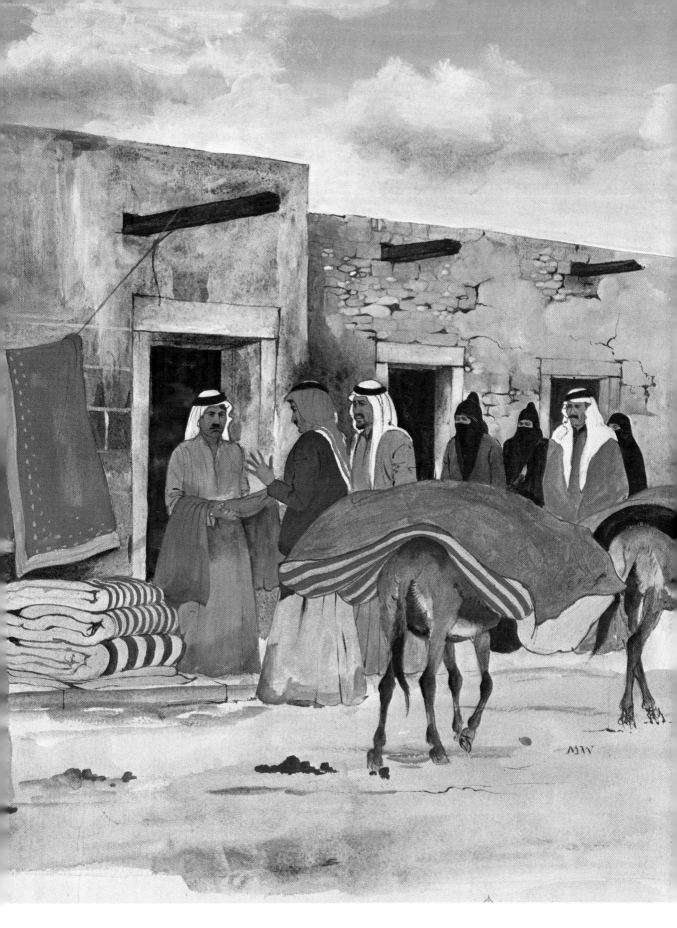

Winter days

When cooler weather arrives, the Bedouin return to the desert—each family on its own, or with a few related families. They can use the old, shallow desert wells since the herds are widely scattered and need water only every five or six days. The camels graze on dry bushes left from the summer. They mate in December and bear their young fourteen months later. (A herder may have half his herd pregnant and half giving milk.) Everyone looks for clouds and waits for rain. The Bedouin say, "There are only two things certain in life: rain and death."

The Bedouin now eat cooked grain or rice with melted fat or dates. Evenings, everyone gathers in one tent for supper. They tell stories, ask riddles, or play games. Sometimes the girls sing.

Singing stories

A favorite entertainment is to listen to poems, stories, or songs that tell of brave deeds of the guests or their families. Most of the men know the poems and join in the chorus. Sometimes a rebaba (a one-stringed fiddle) is used for accompaniment. Rebabas are rare today and are more often made of gasoline cans than of the traditional wood and animal skin.

Finjan

Finjan is a popular game that is played between two teams inside the tent. Twelve coffee cups and a ring or a stone are used. One team hides the ring under a cup and the other team has to guess where it is. If the first guess is right, the team earns twelve points and takes a turn at hiding the ring. The rest of the scoring is complicated. The guessing team is helped by the faces of the children on the other team.

The tents have been resewn for the winter. It can be very cold in the desert; in some areas there is even frost. Fires are needed for warmth and cooking, so the women and children pull up dead roots or bushes for firewood and collect camel dung to burn as fuel.

Sometimes there are winter storms with strong winds and heavy rains. The Bedouin bang the tent pegs firmly into the ground, loosen the ropes, and lower the poles so there will be less wind resistance. When a rope breaks, it sounds like a gunshot. Poles crash down and seams are split by the wind and rain. But it is rare for a tent to collapse completely or for the tent cloth to split. Wet tents are too heavy to move, so the women have to wait for good weather to make repairs.

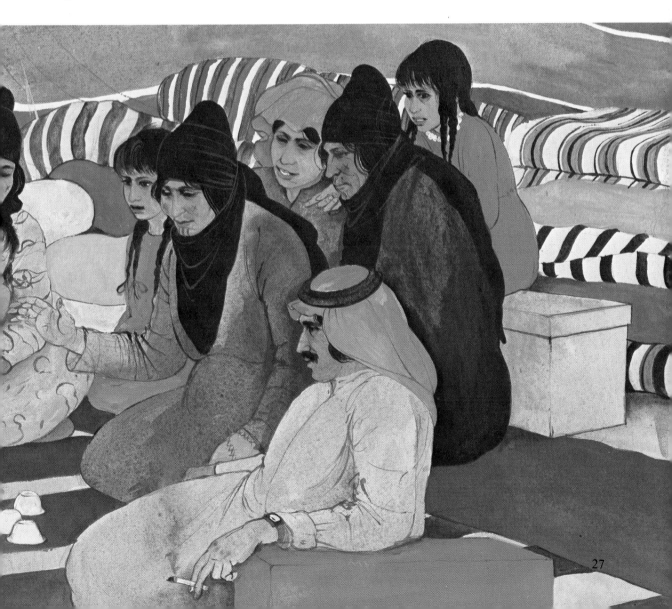

Sheep and goat herders

Sheep shearing
The sheep are sheared by the herders in early summer. They use hand shears. The women of the tribe take the wool or hair they need; then the rest is sold to weavers in the towns. Goats' hair is woven into tent cloth. Sheep's wool is used for rugs, bags, and thread, and for stuffing quilts.

Cheese and yogurt
The women make some of the milk into cream cheese and store it, covered with oil, in jars. Some milk is made into a firmer cheese that can be kept in salted water. Most of the milk is soured and poured into cloth bags. Each bag is put on a flat stone or board with another stone on top so that the whey (the watery part of milk) drains out. After about two weeks the curd (milk solids) is taken out of the bag, salted, shaped into a ball, and put on top of the tent to dry in the sun, away from the dogs. The dried yogurt looks like a white stone. Children are often given a handful of broken bits as a treat. The yogurt can be crushed, mixed with water, and cooked until it thickens. This makes a good sauce to eat with bread or rice. Sheep's milk can also be made into butter. Curdled milk is put into a goatskin butter churn and rocked back and forth for a couple of hours until lumps of butter appear, floating in the thin buttermilk.

Sheep- and goat-herding tribes lead different lives from camel herders. Camels graze on perennial bushes. Sheep and goats graze on annual grass, so they need an area where rain falls more regularly than in the inner desert. Since sheep and goats can't move as quickly as camels and can't go as long without water, their herders stay at the edges of the desert and in the mountain foothills. They go into the desert only in spring, when there is grass for grazing, and the rain pools are full. In summer, they go back to farmland. After the farmers have harvested their crops, the herds of sheep graze on the stubble in the fields, and their droppings fertilize the ground for winter ploughing.

Since they need farmland in summer, sheep and goat herders can't be as independent as camel herders. They form ties to particular villages and also to the camel-herding tribe in whose area they graze in spring. The camel herders protect them from raids by other tribes. In return, they are given sheep or sheep products.

Sheep cost much less than camels, and the herders can earn more money from them. A sheep- or goat-herding family only needs 60 animals to live comfortably, but they can handle 250. This means that a profit can be made in two ways. Most families are paid for tending animals owned by townspeople (who take the lambs and fresh milk), or they enlarge their own herds and sell the extra milk, cheese, butter, wool, and male lambs. In the past, profits were used to buy silver jewelry, farmland, or village houses to rent out and most sheep-herding tribes were considered wealthy by European travelers.

Sheep herders used to have donkeys to carry their tents and belongings from place to place. Their tents had separate side walls so they could be taken apart easily and packed in small bundles. Since sheep move more slowly and graze a smaller area than camels, their herders do not move as often or as far as camel herders. Thus, the women have more time for cooking and weaving.

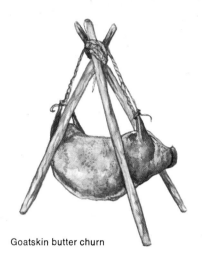

Goatskin butter churn

Milking at sunset

Sheep are milked when they come in after grazing. They are put into two lines facing each other. A rope is threaded over and under their necks. Goats are kept at one end. The women do the milking into saucepans or cans. If there are only a few animals (below) they are milked near the tent.

The new desert

The Bedouin see that as the world changes, they have new opportunities; but they need new skills to use them. Some Bedouin have set out to gain education so that they can take the opportunities offered by oil companies and local governments. Many have trucks and can earn money by keeping sheep in the desert, and by trading and carrying goods. Others have developed pieces of farmland with government help and advice.

Each group of families tries to make use of all opportunities. Older men herd camels; younger men herd sheep and trade and carry goods from one country to another. Among the young men, some may be in military service; some may work for an oil company; and some may be in local government.

Until now, this mixing of old and new lifestyles has worked well, but there are problems. When boys go to school, they have no chance to learn the skills and gain the knowledge of the desert that they need for camel herding.

Some Bedouin give up herding, saying life is hard and the desert dull; others dislike town life and miss their independence. The Bedouin know there will be more changes due to economic and political demands of modern life. But they also believe that when the oil is used up, it will be the Bedouin and their camels who will be able to live in the desert.

Index

Bedouin Legion, 24

Camel Corps, 24
Camel herders, 4, 6–7
Camel raiding, 22, 23
Camels' milk, 8, 28
Celebrations, 14–15
Cheese, 28
Climate, 4, 6, 9, 17, 19, 26–27
Coffee, 21

Donkeys, 4, 29
Drought, 19
Dye, 14

Education, 19, 30
Eggs, 8

Feasts, 14–15
Finjan, 26
Food, 6, 8–9, 14, 17, 26
Free Bedu, 22
Fuel, 11, 13

Games, 26
Goat herders, 4, 28–29
Government, 20–21, 30
Grazing, 6, 9

Henna, 14

Honor, 22

Income, 7, 29
Ishmael, 5

Jerboas, 8, 9

Lifestyles, 30
Locusts, 8–9
Loom, 18

Markets, 24
Marriages, 7, 14–15, 17
Military service, 7, 22, 30
Milk, 8, 28
Milking, 29

Oases, 13, 16
Oil companies, 7, 22

Patterns, woven, 18–19
Plants, 6
Population, 4
Possessions, 22

Raiding, 9, 22, 23
Rain, 4, 6, 9, 17, 19, 26–27
Ramadan, 4
Rebabas, 26
Relatives, 7

Religion, 4
Reputation, 22

Salubba (tribe), 4, 16
Salukis, 8, 9,
Seasons, 8–9, 13, 16–17, 26–27
Sheep herders, 4, 28–29
Sheep shearing, 28
Sheiks, 9, 12–13, 17, 20–21
Singing stories, 26
Spinning, 17
Spring, 8–9
Summer, 13, 16–17

Tattooing, 14
Tents, 10–11, 27, 29
Traders, 16, 24
Tribes, 5
Trucks, 7, 24
Truffles, 8

Water, 12–13
Weaving, 17, 18–19, 28
Weddings, 14–15, 17
Wells, 12–13, 16
Winter, 26–27
Women, 7, 8, 11, 14–15, 17, 18–19, 22

Yogurt, 28
Yokhatan, 5